51 things to make with
Cardboard Boxes

Fiona Hayes

Contents

Basic Equipment

Most of these projects use some or all of the following equipment, so keep these handy:

- PVA glue
- Scissors
- Pencils
- Ruler
- Felt-tip pens
- Paint brushes

Giraffe	4
Crocodile	6
Bubble Cars	8
Pirate Hat	9
Train	10
Flamingo	12
Hippo	14
Lorry	16
Bird House Money Box	18
Fish Tank	20
Angel Fish	22
Christmas Tree	23
Flower Basket	24
Sitting Dog	26
Owl	28
Treasure Chest	29
Butterfly	30
Crab	31
Elephant	32
Tiger	34
Glasses	36
Tractor	37
Tulips	38
Bunny	39
Penguin	40
Row of Houses Desk Tidy	41

Mice and Cheese	42
Crown	44
Spider	45
Snail	46
Octopus	47
Chickens	48
Picnic Basket	50
Cool Cat	51
Robot Mask	52
Reindeer	54
Robot	56
Zebra	58
Whale	59
Bug Bracelet	60
Frog	61
Dinosaur	62
Monster Photo Frame	64
Piglet	66
Ladybird Box	67
Castle	68
Big Mouth Monster	70
Lion	72
Parrot	74
Crane	76
Pirate Ship	78

Giraffe

This gorgeous giraffe will look great in your bedroom. Why not make two and use them as bookends?

1 Cut the end off a cereal box to make the body. Glue two long boxes inside the body box to make legs.

2 Cut off a section from one end of another long box to make the neck.

3 Glue the neck in place, as shown.

4 Cut a wedge from another cereal box, as shown. This top part will be the head. Recycle the rest of the box.

5

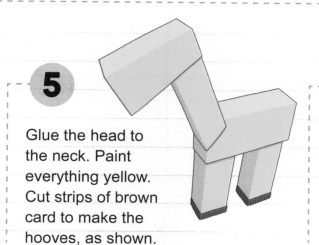

Glue the head to the neck. Paint everything yellow. Cut strips of brown card to make the hooves, as shown.

6

Cut out a pair of ears from card, paint them yellow and glue them in place. Paint on lots of brown spots.

7

Cut a rectangle of thick brown card to cover the snout. Then cut a strip to make the mane and some for the tail. Cut circles of thin card and paint green. Glue the eyes to the green circles and fix to the head. Cut two short pieces of straw for horns. Paint details such as a smile. Add pink to the ears to finish your giraffe.

Handy Hint

For stand-out eyes, cut circles slightly bigger than the googly eyes. Paint them a bright colour and glue the eyes to the circles.

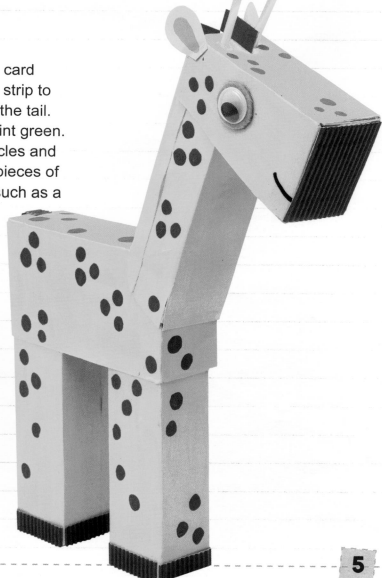

Crocodile

Never smile at a crocodile
– unless it is as cute as this
spotty croc!

You will need

Two cereal boxes
Paint, including green
Thick card
Card
Two googly eyes

1

Cut the corner
off a box.

2

Cut off another two small corners
so that you have three triangles.

3

Cut the sides off another
box, as shown.

4

Paint all the pieces green. Cut a piece of thick
card long enough to fit the crocodile body parts
and paint it. Glue the pieces to the card.

5

Cut two circles of card slightly larger than the googly eyes. Paint them green to match the body. Glue the eyes onto the circles.

6

Glue the circles with eyes to the side of the head.

7

Paint on some spots and nostrils. Snap... snap… your amazing croc is ready!

Handy Hint
Make sure the paint is completely dry before painting on the details.

SNAP

SNAP

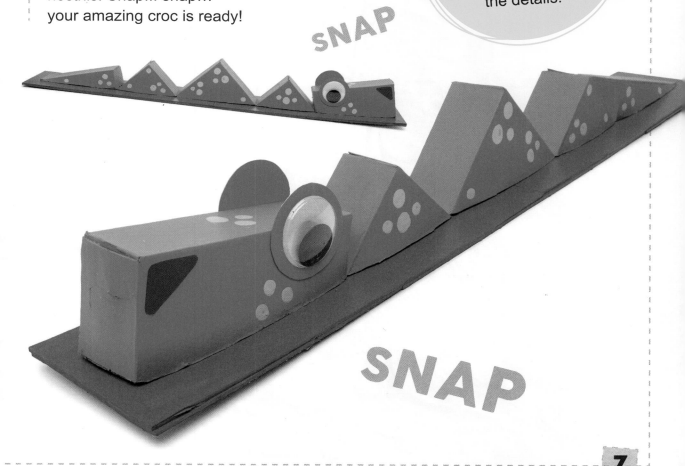

Bubble Cars

Beep! Beep! It's time to take these bubble cars for a drive.

You will need

One round box

Paint, including black, blue and white

Thick card

1 Glue the lid of the round box to the box base. Cut the box in half to make two car bodies.

2 Cut out four circles from thick card. Paint them to look like wheels.

3 Paint the body of each car. When dry, paint on two windows on either side.

4 Glue the wheels in place. Vroom, vroom! These little cars make great toys for rainy days!

Pirate Hat

Arrggh... me hearties! Impress all your friends with your pirate hat!

You will need

Large cereal box
Black paint
White card

1 Cut the corner off a large cereal box.

2 Paint the corner black and recycle the rest.

3 Cut out a circle and a pair of bones from white card to make a skull and crossbones.

4 Draw a face on the skull. Stick the skull and bones to the front of the hat, as shown. Why not make an eye patch to complete your pirate look?

Train

Choo, choo! All aboard! This colourful train will look great on your bedroom windowsill.

1

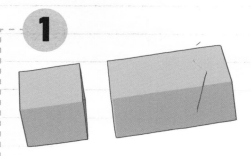

Cut a long box in two, as shown.

2

Glue the shorter piece to the longer piece to make the engine. Glue a square piece of card to the top and another to the front of the engine. Paint the engine.

3

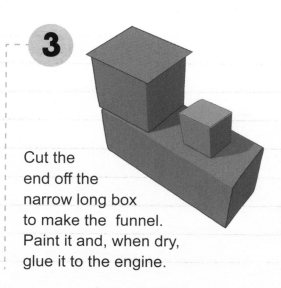

Cut the end off the narrow long box to make the funnel. Paint it and, when dry, glue it to the engine.

4

Paint some mini cereal boxes for the carriages. Paint on some windows.

5

Glue on some bottle tops for the wheels. If you do not have bottle tops, cut out circles of card instead.

6

Glue lengths of ribbon to the base of the carriages and engine to join them.

7

Choo, choo! Your train is ready to leave the station!

CHOO CHOO

Flamingo

What's bright pink, feathery and lives in Africa? A flamingo!

1

Cut the corner off a large cereal box.

2

Cut another triangular section from the rest of the box. Use the corner you cut in step 1 as a template.

3

Slide one section into the other to make a closed triangle for the body. Glue in place and paint pink.

4

Cut out a triangular section from the end of each long box. These will be the neck and legs.

5

Cut the end off a smaller box to make a head. Glue the neck box in place. Paint the neck and part of the head pink. Give the flamingo a white and black beak.

12

6

Glue the neck and head to the body. Paint the legs yellow and glue them to the body, as shown.

7

From card, cut out shapes for the feet and tail, as shown. Paint the feet yellow and the tail pink.

8

Glue the feet in place.

9

Glue the tail in place. Cut some circles from the card so that they are just bigger than the googly eyes. Paint the circles, glue on the eyes and attach to the head. Your pretty flamingo is ready!

Hippo

Hippos love to wade in water
- except for this one!

1

Cut a small box in half, as
shown. This will be the head.

2

Glue two
matchboxes for
eyes to the top of
one of the pieces.
Paint both parts
of the head light
pink on the outside
and dark pink on the inside.

3

Glue the backs of the boxes
together, making sure you have
the mouth open. Use some
paper clips to hold the pieces
in place until they are dry.

4

Paint another box light pink.
Glue this to the back of the head.

5

Paint four matchboxes light pink and
glue them to the bottom for feet.

6

Cut out a pair of ears from card and paint light pink, with dark pink in the inside.

7

Handy Hint

If you do not have pink paint, you could mix red and white to get the right shade.

Cut some circles from the card so that they are just bigger than the googly eyes. Paint the circles green, glue on the eyes and attach to the head. Glue on the ears. Cut out some teeth from the white card and glue them inside the mouth.

8

Paint on some spots, nostrils and toenails. Say hello to your cheeky hippo!

Lorry

Vrooom... Beep, beep! Watch out. This huge lorry is carrying a heavy load!

1

Cut the top off a box at an angle, as shown. The large piece will be the trailer of your lorry.

2

Find a box the same height as your trailer for the driver's cab. Glue a small box between the cab and trailer, as shown. Paint all pieces.

3

Cut some panels from the corrugated card. Paint them and glue them to the trailer.

4

Cut out eight circles from thick card and paint them black. Glue some smaller circles of shiny card to the centres.

5

Glue the wheels in place. Cut out some windows from card and glue to the cab.

BEEP BEEP

Handy Hint
Use clothes pegs to hold pieces in place while you wait for glue to dry.

6

Glue on two bottle tops for headlights and a grill from shiny card. This super lorry is ready for the road.

Bird House Money Box

Count your pennies and save all your money in this colourful bird house.

You will need

Tall box
Paint
Thick card
One straw

1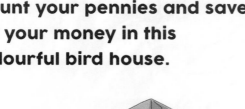

Cut the top flaps off a tall box.

2

Cut slits in each corner. Fold in the edges to make a triangle at the front and back.

3

Glue one of the rectangular flaps to the edge of the triangle, as shown. Cut off the other flap.

4

Use a pencil to start a hole for your scissors. Cut out an entrance hole, as shown. Paint the box a lovely bright colour.

5

Cut a rectangle of thick card and fold it in half to make the roof. Paint it a contrasting colour to the bird house.

6

Glue one side of the roof to the top of the box. Leave the other side so you can open the box to get your money.

7

Make a hole with a pencil in the front of the box. Glue in a piece of straw for a perch. Now you can start saving your money for something special!

Handy Hint

Make sure the entrance hole in your bird house is bigger than your biggest coin.

Fish Tank

If you've always wanted a fish tank, make this fun and colourful water world!

1

Cut a large, rectangular hole in the front of the tissue box. Paint the inside of the box a light blue and the outside of the box a different shade of blue. This is your fish tank.

2

On thick card, draw a triangle with a smaller triangle overlapping it, as shown. Then cut it out. This will be one of your fish.

3

Use the template from step 2 to cut out four more fish. Paint the fish bright colours. Glue an eye on to each fish.

4

Use a pencil to make five holes in the top of your fish tank. Push a bendy straw through each hole, with the bend at the top.

5

Glue your fish to the
straws. Glue them at
different heights and
facing different directions.

6

To make seaweed, cut out some wavy
pieces of thick card and paint them
green. Glue them to the inside of the tank.
Twist the straws to make your fish swim.

glub
glub

Angel Fish

This lovely fish will make your house look heavenly!

You will need

One cereal box
Paint
Yellow card
One googly eye

1

Cut the corner off a box.

2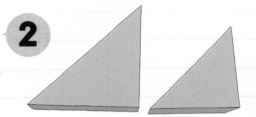

Cut a smaller corner from the other side of the box.

3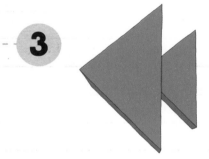

Glue the smaller triangle into the larger one to make a fish shape. Paint the fish and leave it to dry.

4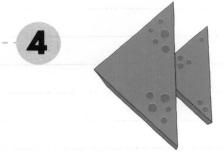

Paint on spots or stripes.

5

Cut out a circle from yellow card, slightly bigger than the googly eye. Glue the eye to the circle and then glue it to the fish. This colourful fish will brighten up any house.

Christmas Tree

1

Cut the corner off a box.

2

Cut two corners off another cereal box so that all three triangles are different sizes.

3

Slot the triangles into each other, from the smallest to the biggest. Glue them in place and paint green.

4

Paint a narrow box brown to make the trunk. Glue it to the inside of the bottom triangle.

5

Paint on lots of bright baubles.

6

Cut out a star from the thick card, paint it yellow and glue it to the top of your tree. Put your tree on a window ledge to add some festive cheer to your room at Christmas time.

Flower Basket

This flower basket will make a perfect gift for your family and friends. Or maybe just for you!

You will need

One cereal box
Paint
Corrugated card
Card
Nine bendy straws
Tissue paper, including green

1 Cut the sides away from a cereal box, as shown.

2 Cut away the top to make it curved, as shown.

3 Use a pencil to make a hole for your scissors. Cut out the middle part of the sides to give your basket handles.

4 Paint the handles and cover the bottom part of your basket with corrugated card. Paint the corrugated card to match the handles.

5

Cut out nine circles from card to make flowers. Cut slits around the edges to create petals. Paint the flowers lovely bright colours.

6

Add a ball of yellow or orange tissue paper to the centre of each flower. Glue a bendy straw to each flower to make a stem.

7

Arrange the flowers in the basket. Push some green tissue paper around the flowers to keep them in place. Your beautiful flowers will brighten up anyone's day!

Handy Hint

If you do not have yellow or orange tissue paper, paint yellow or orange circles instead.

Sitting Dog

This dog will make the perfect pet. Your doggy friend will always sit and beg for attention!

1

Cut the corner off a cereal box, as shown. Keep the large piece for the body and recycle the rest.

2

Cut out the head from another cereal box, as shown.

3

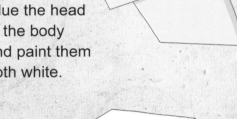

Glue the head to the body and paint them both white.

4

Cut out a pair of legs and a tail from thick card, as shown. Paint them white.

5

Cut a slit in the back of the body and slide in the tail. Glue to hold in place. Glue the legs to the sides.

6

Cut out a pair of ears from card and paint them black.

7

Glue the ears in place. Paint a large black patch on your dog's face.

Handy Hint

You can paint on a nose if you do not have a bottle top.

8

Add some grey spots. Glue on a bottle top for the nose and a pair of googly eyes. Add a friendly smile. Woof, woof!

WOOF
WOOF
WOOF

owl

You will need

Round box
Paint
Two bottle tops
Card
Thick card
Two googly eyes

1

Glue the lid to the base of the box. Paint it a bright colour.

2

Glue two bottle tops so that they stick out off the edge of the box. Cut out two circles from the card so that they are just bigger than the eyes. Glue the eyes to the circles and then the circles to the bottle tops.

3

Cut out a circle of card, paint it and glue it to the front.

4

Cut out an angled piece of card, as shown. Paint it the same colour as the body. Glue to the back of the owl at the top.

5

Cut out a semi-circle from thick card for feet. Cut out a diamond from card for the beak. Paint them yellow.

6

Glue on the beak. Glue the semi-circle to the bottom of the box at the back so your owl can stand up. Be a wise owl and decorate your bookshelf!

Treasure Chest

You will need

One shoebox   Yellow card

Paint, including brown   Small boxes

Shiny paper

1

Paint a shoebox brown.

2

Cut some long narrow strips of yellow card and glue them to the top and front of the box.

3

Cut out a lock from the yellow card.

4

Cut a thin strip of card and glue it to make a loop through the top of the lock. Paint on a key hole.

5

Glue the lock to the box by gluing on the loop. Add some handles of yellow card to either end. Paint some nails on the chest.

6

Cover some small boxes with shiny paper to make treasure. You could also use your box to keep your favourite things safe.

Butterfly

 1

Cut the corners off two thin boxes to make the butterfly's wings.

 2

Paint the outside of the wings a pretty colour and the insides a contrasting colour.

3

Place the pieces together so that the ends touch, as shown.

 4

Paint a matchbox and glue it on top of the wings for the butterfly's body.

5

Add some spots on the wings.

6

Glue some pieces of straw to the back of the body for antennae. Add two googly eyes and a little smile. You could tie a loop of ribbon to the butterfly and hang it from your ceiling.

30

Crab

You will need

One round box

Brown and orange paint

Thick card

Two googly eyes

1

Glue the lid to the base of the box. Cut in half. Paint one half orange.

2

From card, cut two circles slightly bigger than the googly eyes. Paint the circles orange and glue on the eyes.

3

Glue the eyes to the top of the box.

4

Cut out a pair of claws and six legs from thick card. Paint the claws brown and the legs orange.

5

Glue the claws to the front of the box. Glue the legs to the inside of the box, so that there are four at the back and two at the front.

6

Add some spots and a mouth. Why not put your crab with the fish from page 22 to make an aquarium?

31

Elephant

Elephants live in a herd
so why don't you make
your elephant a friend?

You will need

Two cereal boxes
Grey, pink, black and white paint
White and purple card
Two googly eyes

1

Cut a triangle
in one corner
of a cereal box. Cut another
triangle on the opposite side.
Fold both triangles away from the
box, as shown. Cut at the corner
from A to B, as shown.

2

Fold the
triangles and
flaps into the box.
Glue to hold in place.

3

Cut out a head shape
from the box, as shown.

4

Cut out a
semi-circle
from another
box to make the body.

Handy Hint

If you cut the wrong
bit in step 1, do not
worry – you can
always tape it
back together.

5

Paint both boxes grey.
Glue the head to the body.

6

Cut out a pair of ears from card. Paint them grey with pink in the middle.

7

Glue the ears in place.

8

Cut out a tail and pair of tusks from the card. Paint the tail grey. Cut out purple circles and glue the eyes to them. Glue on the tail, tusks and eyes. Paint on some spots and toenails to finish your elephant.

CUTE

Tiger

Grrrr! Tigers are stripey, orange and fluffy. But, beware, these cats are anything but cute!

You will need

One cereal box

Orange, black, white and pink paint

Card

Two googly eyes

One bottle top

1

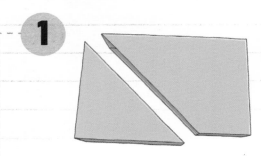

Cut the corner off a cereal box.

2

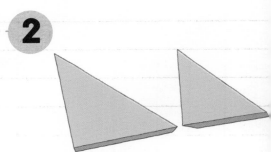

Cut another smaller corner out of the cereal box.

3

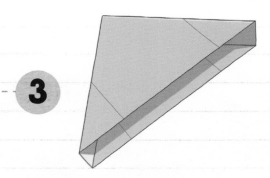

Cut four slits in the larger triangle, as shown. This will be the tiger's body.

4

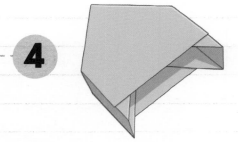

Fold the ends into the middle and glue to hold in place so you have a shape that looks like a house. Cut off any bits that stick out from the bottom so you have a flat base.

5

Glue the smaller triangle on top of the bigger one. Paint the tiger orange with a white tummy and muzzle.

6

Cut out a tail and a pair of ears from card. Paint them as shown.

7

Glue the ears and tail in place. Paint black stripes on to the tiger's body.

GRRR GRRR

8

Glue on a pair of googly eyes and a bottle top for the nose. Add a mouth to finish off your tiger. Now, your tiger is ready to roar!

Glasses

1 Unfold the boxes
and cut off the tops.

2 Glue the tops together so
that they overlap slightly.
Paint them lovely bright
colours – you could add
some patterns, too.

3 Cut out a pair of arms
from thick card and paint
them to match the tops.

4 Turn the glasses over
and glue the arms to
the back, as shown.

5 Bend the arms into
the middle. Your
cool glasses are
ready to wear.

Tractor

Time to get busy on the farm with your tractor. Chug! Chug!

1

Glue the square box to the top of the long box. Paint them both red.

2

Paint the large lids black with white centres to make the back wheels. Cut out two small circles from thick card and paint them. These are the front wheels.

3

Glue the wheels to the tractor, as shown.

4

Cut out some windows from the card. Glue them to the tractor.

5

Draw a driver and some passengers in the windows. Cut out a rectangle of card and paint it silver to make a grill to attach to the front. Glue the toothpaste tube lid to make the chimney. Your tractor is ready to go!

Tulips

Tulips are beautiful, brightly coloured flowers. Why not make a bunch of these pretty blooms and put them in a vase?

1 To make two tulips, glue the lid to the base of the round box. Cut it in half.

2 Cut out small triangles to give each half a zig-zag edge.

3 Paint your tulips different colours. Paint the insides too.

4 Use a pencil to make a hole in the bottom of each tulip. Glue a straw into each hole for a stem.

5 Repeat steps 1 to 4 with the second box to make two more tulips. They will make a lovely gift for someone special.

Bunny

You will need

One chocolate box

Card

Brown, pink and cream paint

Two googly eyes

1

Paint the box brown.

2

Cut out a pair of feet and ears from card. Paint the feet brown and the ears brown, with pink in the middle.

3

Cut out a dome shape from card for the bunny's tummy. Paint it cream.

4

Glue the ears, feet and tummy in place.

5

Glue on some googly eyes and draw on a nose and a smile. If you have smaller boxes, you can make some baby bunnies.

39

Penguin

You will need

Chocolate box
Black and blue paint
Thick card
White and yellow card
Two googly eyes

1

Paint the box black.

2

Cut out a pair of wings from thick card and paint them black.

3

Next, cut out a dome shape from white card for the penguin's tummy.

4

Glue the wings and tummy in place.

5

Cut out two circles from the white card. Paint them blue and glue the eyes to them. Glue the eyes in place.

6

Cut out a beak from yellow card and glue it under the eyes. Your penguin is ready to swim.

Row of Houses Desk Tidy

1 You will need two boxes the same size for each house. To make each house, cut off the corner of one of the boxes, for the roof.

2 Fold the top flaps inside and glue to hold in place. This will make it stronger when you take the roof on and off. Paint the house.

3 Glue some corrugated card to the roof and paint it.

4 Now repeat steps 1 to 3 with the other boxes, but have some solid boxes, with closed tops, between the open ones. Glue the row of houses onto a strip of thick card.

5 Put the roofs on the open-ended boxes. Cut out rectangles for windows and glue them to your houses. Put all your stationery in the houses to keep your desk neat and tidy.

Mice and Cheese

Do mice love cheese? You bet! And you'll love these little mice and the cheese once you've made them!

1

To make each mouse, cut the corner off a box so that the cut piece has three edges. This will be the body.

2

Paint the body grey.

3

Cut out a pair of ears and a tail from pink card.

4

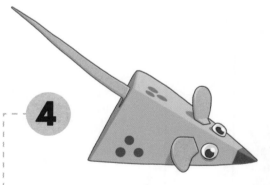

Glue the tail and ears to the body, paint on a black nose and some spots. Glue on a pair of googly eyes. Repeat the steps to make another mouse, but paint it a darker colour.

5

Cut the top off another box, at an angle – you need the small piece for your wedge of cheese. Recycle the rest.

6

Paint the cheese yellow. Paint on some crescents with a darker yellow to look like holes.

7

Place your mice on the cheese and let them nibble away!

Handy Hint

Have a game of cat and mouse when you make these mice and the cat from page 51.

EEK

Crown

This crown is fit for a Queen... or a King!

1

Gently flatten a cereal box and cut it in half.

You will need

One cereal box

Paint, including yellow and gold

Card

Glitter

2

Cut out a row of triangles around one edge of the top half.

3

Paint your crown yellow.

4

Cut a strip of card to fit around the bottom of the crown. Paint it gold and glue it in place.

5

Cut out some circles from card and paint them jewel-like colours. Add some glitter to the centres.

6

Glue the jewels to the tips of the crown and it will be fit for royalty!

spider

1

Paint your box black. This will be the spider's body.

2

Cut out eight legs from thick card. Paint them black.

3

Glue the legs to the base of the body.

4

Turn over your spider and bend the legs, as shown.

5

Cut two circles from thick card. Make them slightly bigger than the googly eyes. Paint the circles black and glue on the eyes.

6

Glue the eyes to the body. Paint on spots. Is your spider friendly or scary?

Snail

1

Paint the lid and base of a round box.

3

Cut out a body for your snail from thick card. Paint it then glue the body onto the cut-out part of the box base.

2

Cut off part of the rim from the base of the box, as shown.

4

Glue the lid to the base, so that the body is trapped between the lid and the base. Paint on some spots.

5

Use the tip of a pencil to make a hole in the head. Insert a piece of bendy straw into the hole for the horns.

6

Glue some pompoms to the horns. Draw on a smile and a pair of googly eyes. Cute!

Octopus

You will need

Hexagonal
(six-sided) box

Green and pink paint

Card

Two googly eyes

1

Paint the top of your box
green and the underside
pink. This will be the body.

2

Cut out eight
legs from card.
Paint them green
on one side and
pink on the other.

3

Glue the legs to the base
of the body, pink side up.

4

Cut two circles from card.
Make them slightly bigger than
the googly eyes. Paint the circles
green and glue on the eyes.

5

Turn your octopus over and
gently curl his legs upwards.
Glue on his eyes.

6

Paint on lots of
spots and a smile.
Your octopus is
ready – why not put
him in your bathroom?

Chickens

Cluck, cluck! Who's the cutest chicken on the farm? I think these two are in the running!

You will need

Two cereal boxes

Brown, yellow, white and grey paint

Red and yellow card

Four googly eyes

1

For each chicken, cut the corner off a box, making the base curved.

2

Cut another smaller corner, with a straight base.

3

Paint the curved corner brown for the body, and the small one yellow for the feet. Glue the feet to the inside of the body.

4

Cut out two crests from red card.

5

Cut out a
beak from
yellow card.

6

Glue the
crests and
beak in place.

7

Add a pair of googly eyes and
some grey spots. Repeat the
steps to make the second
chicken, but paint its body
white instead of brown.

Handy Hint

Always allow
the glue to dry
completely before
moving your
model.

CLUCK CLUCK

Picnic Basket

You will need

One shoebox with a detachable lid

Paint, including green

Thick card

1 Cut two slits in either side of the shoebox lid.

2 Fold the lid back on itself along each slit. Use the edge of a table to make a straight crease.

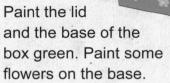

3 Paint the lid and the base of the box green. Paint some flowers on the base.

4 Cut and fold a strip of thick card to make a handle. Check that it fits over the lid of the box.

5 Glue the middle of the lid to the base – you should still be able to open the lid from each end.

6 Decorate the lid and glue the handle in place. Happy picnicking!

Cool Cat

You will need

Chocolate box

Orange, yellow and pink paint

Thick card

White card

Pink felt

Two googly eyes

1 Paint the box yellow.

2 Cut out a pair of ears and a tail from thick card and paint yellow.

3 Paint the middle of the ears pink. Glue them and the tail in place.

4 Cut out a dome shape from white card for the cat's tummy. Glue it to the front of the box. Paint some stripes onto the rest of the box.

5 Cut out a semi-circle of pink felt for the cat's nose. Glue the nose and a pair of eyes to the face. Draw on a mouth. If you have some smaller boxes, you can make some cute kittens.

51

Robot Mask

Robots at the ready! Look out, here we come! Make this awesome robot mask and take the world by storm.

1 Cut the back off a cereal box. Paint the front of the box blue.

2 Glue the lids to the bases of two round boxes. Paint the boxes red. Cover two small boxes with shiny card. Glue one to each of the round boxes.

3 Glue the small boxes to either side of the mask, as shown. Use the end of a pencil to make a hole for your scissors, then cut out two circles on the front of the box for eye holes. Paint white circles around them.

4 Cut the lid of a round box in half to leave two semi-circles. Glue these to some strips of thick card and paint them yellow. Glue them to the top of the mask.

5

Add some coloured bottle tops above the eyes.

6

To make the mouth, cover a small box with shiny card and glue it in place. Your robot mask is ready to wear.

ROBOTS RULE

Handy Hint

To keep your mask in place, make holes on either side of the mask and attach some elastic.

Reindeer

This amazing reindeer is every bit as cute as Rudolf! Have fun making a whole team of reindeer to pull your sleigh.

1 Cut out the body shape from a cereal box, as shown.

2 Cut the end off a small box to make a cube for the reindeer's neck.

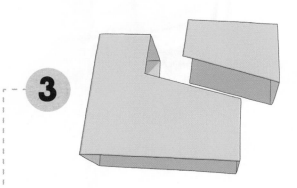

3 Cut the corner from another cereal box for the head.

4 Glue the neck to the body and then glue on the head. Paint the whole reindeer brown.

5

Cut out a pair of ears and a pair of antlers. Paint them all brown.

6

Glue on the ears and antlers. Add a bottle top for the nose.

7

Paint on some white spots. Add pink to the middle of the ears. Glue on a pair of eyes and a pompom for the tail. Draw on a smile and your reindeer is ready.

CUTE

Robot

Make an army of super-cool robots to take over the world! (Or just your house.)

1

Paint two different sized boxes. Then glue the smaller box to the top of the larger box.

2

Cover two toilet rolls with corrugated card. Glue them to the base of the large box to make legs.

3

Next, paint two matchboxes and glue them to the toilet rolls. These will be the feet.

4

To make each arm, cut the end off a sweet tube and paint it. Cut out two circles of card and paint them. Use a split pin to attach the open end of the arms to the circles of coloured card.

5

Glue the arms to either side of the body, as shown. You will be able to move the arms up and down.

6

Use the end of a pencil to make two holes at the top of the head. Insert two small pieces of bendy straw. Cut a rectangle of shiny paper for the front and glue in place.

7

Glue on some bottle tops for the eyes and ears. Add some googly eyes to the inside of the bottle tops and a strip of painted corrugated card for a mouth.

8

Glue some tube tops and coloured card circles to the robot's tummy to decorate it. Your robot is complete – have lots of fun playing with it!

zebra

1

Cut out the body from one of the boxes, as shown.

2

Cut the end off the small box to make a cube for the neck.

3

Cut the corner from the other box for the head.

4

Glue the neck to the body and then glue on the head. Paint the zebra white with black stripes and a black nose.

5

Cut out a pair of ears, a mane and a tail from black card. Glue them in place.

6

Cut out some circles of card that are slightly bigger than the googly eyes. Glue the eyes to the circles and add them to the zebra. Paint on a mouth and two nostrils.

Whale

You'll have a whale of a time making this beautiful sea giant!

You will need

One shoebox with a detachable lid
Paint
One cardboard box
Card
Two googly eyes

1 Paint the base of the shoebox dark blue on the outside and pink on the inside. Cut the end of the base diagonally, as shown.

2 Paint the lid pale blue on the outside and pink on the inside. Glue the base to the lid so that it is open, as shown.

3 Cut out a heart-shaped corner from the other box. This will be the tail.

4 Paint the tail dark blue and glue it to the body.

5 Cut out some circles of card. Paint a contrasting colour. Glue the eyes to the circles and attach to the whale's head. Paint on some spots to finish your whale.

Bug Bracelet

You will need

Four matchboxes

Ring from finished sticky tape

Paint

Black felt

Eight googly eyes

1

Paint your matchboxes different colours.

2

Cut six narrow strips of black felt and glue to the base of each box for legs.

3

Paint spots or stripes on the top of the boxes. Glue two eyes to each bug.

4

Paint the cardboard sticky tape ring green.

5

Glue the bugs to the outside of the cardboard ring to make a bracelet. To make a ring for your finger instead, glue a small loop of cardboard to the back of a bug.

Frog

You will need

**One box with
a hinged lid**

Thick card

Green and yellow paint

Two googly eyes

1

Cut out a semi-circle of card the same width as the box. Glue the semi-circle to the front of the lid and paint green, as shown.

2

Paint on a yellow tummy.

3

Cut out two small semi-circles and paint them green. Glue them to the front of the box for the feet.

4

From card, cut two circles slightly bigger than the eyes. Paint the circles green and glue on the eyes.

5

Bend the bottom of the card circles and glue the eyes to the top of the box.

6

Paint on yellow spots and a happy smile. Be careful your frog doesn't hop away!

Dinosaur

Dinosaurs lived around 230 million years ago but you can make this super dino today!

1

Cut a corner off the large cereal box for the dinosaur's body. Keep the rest of the box, to make a tail and legs.

2

Cut a long triangle from the left-over pieces of cereal box to make the dinosaur tail.

3

Cut a slot halfway up one side of the body, and slide in the tail. Glue to hold in place.

4

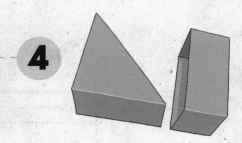

Cut a corner and end section from the small cereal box to make the head and neck.

5

Cut two small slits at one end of the triangle from step 4, and fold in. Glue in place. This is the snout.

6

Glue the neck into the head.

7

Cut four triangles from corrugated card for the legs.

Handy Hint
Use a piece of card as a spatula to spread the glue.

8

Glue the head, neck and legs in place. Let them dry. Paint and decorate the dinosaur. Glue some small triangles from felt for its spine. Use two felt circles for the googly eyes and fix in place. Now your dinosaur is ready to roar!

Monster Photo Frame

You will need

One tissue box
Paint
Thin card
Two googly eyes
White felt

1

Open one end of the tissue box. If the front has any plastic in it, remove it now.

Handy Hint

You can use thin card if you don't have felt.

2

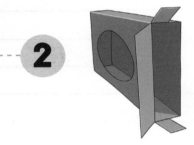

To make a slot to slide your photo through, cut off one of the long flaps and around 1 centimetre off the small flaps on either side. Glue the remaining parts back together.

3

Cut two circles from the card. They need to be slightly larger than the googly eyes.

4

Paint the circles and your box.

5

Once dry, fold the bottom part of the card circles, as shown. Then glue the eyes in place.

6

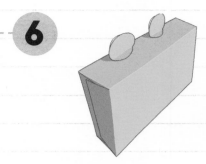

Glue the folded edge of each circle to the long side of the tissue box, with the eyes facing forwards.

7

Cut lots of teeth from felt and glue them around the inside of the mouth. Decorate your monster, then choose a cheeky little monster photo to pop inside!

BOO!

Piglet

1 Glue the lid and base of one box together. Then cut the base and lid from the other box, as shown. Glue the larger piece's lid and base together but do not glue the small pieces. Paint all pieces pink.

2 Glue the two small pieces to the base of the whole box. These will be the pig's trotters.

3 Cut out a pair of ears from card and paint them. Glue the ears to the top of the head, and fold the tips forward. Glue the head to the pig's body, as shown.

4 Paint a bottle top pink and glue it to the pig's face.

5 Wrap a strip of pink card around a pencil to make a curly tail.

6 From blue card, cut two circles slightly bigger than the eyes. Glue them, the googly eyes and the tail in place. Paint on nostrils.

Ladybird Box

You will need

One round box

Thick card

Black, red and blue paint

Two googly eyes

Two split pins

1

Cut the lid from the round box into slightly less than half. Recycle the bigger piece. Paint the smaller piece and the base of the box black.

2

Draw around the base of the box onto thick card. Cut the circle out, then cut it in half. These will be the wings. Paint them red with black spots. Make one end black, for the head.

3

Make a hole with the tip of a pencil through the wing and the lid section. Use a split pin to attach together. Repeat with the other wing.

4

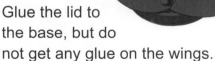

Glue the lid to the base, but do not get any glue on the wings.

5

From thick card, cut out circles that are slightly bigger than the eyes. Paint them blue and glue on a pair of googly eyes. Glue the eyes to the ladybird.

67

Castle

If you like stories with knights and princesses or dungeons and dragons, you'll love this amazing castle!

You will need

About seven or eight different sized boxes, including one with an opening flap

Paint

Card

Two straws

1

Paint the boxes and leave to dry.

2

The box with the opening flap will be the drawbridge. Paint the inside of this a contrasting colour.

3

Glue all your boxes together in a castle shape.

4

Cut some narrow strips of card. Then cut small notches along one edge of the strips of card.

5

Glue these strips of card to the top edges of the boxes, as shown.

6

Cut out some windows from card. Paint and glue in place.

7

Make some flags by cutting and painting card. Then glue them to short pieces of straws, as shown.

8

In the top of the towers, make a hole for each flag. Glue in place. Your castle is ready to play with!

Handy Hint

Practise arranging your castle before you glue the boxes together.

Big Mouth Monster

This monster has a BIG MOUTH. Make your monster scary or funny - you decide!

You will need

One box with an opening flap

Paint

Two matchboxes

White card

Three googly eyes

1 You need a box with an opening flap on it. Paint it a bright colour on the outside and a different colour on the inside.

2 Paint two matchboxes. These will be the feet.

3 Glue the monster's body to the feet. Make sure the flap is at the front.

4 Cut two narrow strips of white card. Then cut out triangles along one edge of the strips. These will be the teeth.

5

Glue the teeth to the inside of the top of the mouth, as shown.

6

Cut three circles from card. They should be slightly bigger than the googly eyes. Paint the circles the same colour as the body, and glue on the eyes.

7

Glue the eyes to the top of the box. Paint on some spots and toenails. Your monster is ready to scare your friends!

Lion

Lions live in groups called a pride. How many lions will you make?

You will need

Two round boxes
Yellow and pink paint
Thick card
Brown and green felt
Two googly eyes
Black bottle top

1

Glue the lid and base of one box together. Then cut the base and lid from the other box, as shown. Glue the larger piece's lid and base together but do not glue the small pieces. Paint all pieces yellow.

2

Cut out a pair of ears and a tail from thick card. Paint as shown.

3

Glue the ears to the top of the round box.

4

Cut out a strip of brown felt. Cut a fringe along one edge to make the lion's mane.

5

Glue the mane around the back edge of the head. Glue the head to the large piece of the cut box, as shown.

6 Glue the two small pieces of the cut box to the body for the paws.

7 Stick a piece of the fringed felt to the end of the tail. Glue this and a bottle-top nose in place.

8 Cut green circles of felt that are slightly bigger than the googly eyes. Glue them to the lion's face, and glue the eyes to them. Add a smile and ROAR... your lion is ready to play.

ROAR ROAR

Parrot

Who's a clever boy, then?
This parrot and its friend!
Make these jungle birds and
put them in your bedroom.

1

For each parrot, cut the side of a box as shown. You need the top part for the parrot's body.

2

Cut a curved corner off another box to make the parrot's head.

3

Paint the pieces and glue them together.

4

Cut out a beak from thick card and paint it black.

5

Cut a slit in the front of the head, slide in the beak and glue to hold.

6

Cut out a pair of wings
from thick card and paint feathers,
as shown.

7

Glue on the wings. Cut out two
circles from the card and glue them
to either side of the head. Glue on
a pair of googly eyes, as shown.

8

Paint around the eyes and add detail
to the beak. Paint the narrow box
brown. Glue the box into the middle of
the body so the parrot has a perch.
Repeat all the steps to make
the second parrot – why
not paint it in different
colours?

**Handy
Hint**
Cut the perches
at different heights
so the birds look
like they are on
different trees.

Crane

Building sites are busy, busy, busy! Can you build a crane to help lift the heavy loads?

You will need

Small cereal box	Eight bottle tops
Paint	Card
Three narrow boxes	Two bendy straws
Corrugated card	

1

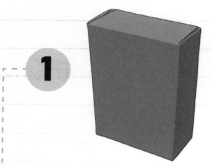

Paint a small cereal box.

2

Paint two narrow boxes in a different colour. Glue a strip of corrugated card around four edges of each box, as shown.

3

Cut the end of another narrow box, as shown. Paint it to match the other boxes in step 2.

4

Glue the narrow boxes to the blue box, as shown.

5

Glue on the bottle tops for the track rollers and the crane winch.

6

Cut out some windows from card and glue onto the cab. Add a dot of paint for the screw on the winch.

7

Wrap two small pieces of card around two short pieces of bendy straw. Paint the card to match the straws.

8

Make a hole in the base of the crane arm with the tip of a pencil. Glue the straws in place to make the crane grab. Get ready, steady, build!

Pirate Ship

Arrggh! Calling all pirates! Prepare to set sail on the seven seas in this pirate ship.

You will need

One cereal box

Two boxes of different sizes

Brown, yellow, blue, red, black and white paint

Card, including grey

Thick card

1

Carefully open the ends of a large cereal box. Cut off the flaps, as shown.

2

Cut a slit down one edge and fold back the side at an angle. Repeat on all four of the base corners.

3

Fold the corners in and bring the base and top sides together. Glue to hold in place. This will give you a ship-shaped base.

4

Paint the shaped box brown.

5

Paint two different sized boxes brown and glue them to the large box, as shown.

6

Cut out lots of circles of card and paint as portholes. Glue them to the sides.

7

Cut out some sails from card and paint them. Cut out some narrow strips of thick card for the masts and paint yellow. Glue the sails to the masts.

8

Fold a piece of grey card in half and cut out an anchor. Glue the anchor to the ship.

9

Make slits in the top box with a pencil and glue in the masts. Your pirate ship is ready to sail – arrggh, me hearties, land ahoy!

Handy Hint
Why not design your own flag to fly on your pirate ship?

Quarto is the authority on a wide range of topics.
Quarto educates, entertains and enriches the lives of
our readers—enthusiasts and lovers of hands-on living.
www.quartoknows.com

Design and Editorial: Calcium
Photography: Michael Wicks
Illustration: Tom Connell
With thanks to our wonderful models Islah, Ethan and Ania.

First published in the UK in 2016
by QED Publishing
Part of The Quarto Group
The Old Brewery, 6 Blundell Street
London, N7 9BH

A catalogue record for this book is available from the British Library.

ISBN 978 1 78493 556 6

Printed in China